Poems

From Travels In Three Countries

By

JAMES RAY ELLERSTON

Ellermus Publications

2406 18th Avenue North

Fort Dodge, Iowa

50501-7805

USA

Copyright © 2005, 2007, 2009, 2011, 2013, 2014

By James R Ellerston

ISBN Number: 978-1500522476

All rights reserved, including the right to reproduce this book or portions thereof in any form whatsoever.

Book design and Typesetting by Keegan Joël VanDevender,

Pella, Marion County, Iowa

50219 USA

Charleroi.Weebly.Com

Printed in the United States of America

ABOUT THE AUTHOR

James R. Ellerston, born in 1950, is a poet, historian, musician, father and husband who has traveled nine times to Europe, as well as western Canada and the United States including Alaska and Hawaii. He was a music educator for thirty-three years in Iowa, performing on violin and viola in community ensembles. He earned a B.A. from Central College (Pella, Iowa) in 1972, an M.S. in Education from Bemidji State University in 1976 and an additional B.A. in Management and Personnel from Buena Vista University in 1987. He resides in Fort Dodge, Iowa and has spent part of each summer for the past fifty-nine years at his cabin on Ten Mile Lake near Hackensack, Minnesota. He married his editor and wife Shelley in 1978.

James R Ellerston

TABLE OF CONTENTS

Part One: Giacomo a Italia

Writing...14

Be On The Bus In The Morning.................15

Lingua Italiana.....................................17

Desposizione Dalla Croce.........................19

Coliseum: Photo and Song........................20

Equestrian Salvation...............................21

Pisa..23

Child Workouts.....................................24

Po Valley...25

No Separation of Church and State in Milano..26

Baveno On Lago Maggiore.......................27

Monte Tamaro Svizzera (1961 m)...............29

Verona..30

Verona: the House of Juliet and Romeo.........31

Venizia..32

Ravenna (The Souvenir)...........................35

Ravenna (Caffè Farini).............................36

Umbria..37

Under the Umbrian Sun...........................39

Valley Highway View of Monte Cassino......41

Pompeii...42

Seggiovia Monte Solaro (Anacapri)...........43

Axel Munthe and Villa San Michele...........45

Circumnavigation of the Isola di Capri......46

Moving Forward With the Crowd...........49

Leaving Sorrento Behind.......................51

On the Way to Roma...........................55

Rome by Night.................................57

Five Haiku......................................60

Tour's End......................................61

Apartment in the Roma sky...................62

Apartment Life 2.............................64

Haiku a Roma.................................65

More Haiku Two..............................66

Even More Haiku Three......................67

Backyard.......................................68

Museo di Montecassiono.....................69

Italian Meal in a Farm House................71

At the House of Renato Valeri...............73

Even More Haiku from Italy Four...........75

A Parody of the poet John Keats 76

Poems From Travels In Three Countries

One of Fagin's boys.....................................77

Three coins in the fountain.........................79

Fruit farm visit..81

Sicily-Rome American Cemetery and Memorial..82

Even More Haiku Five................................84

Galleria Borghese a Roma...........................85

A Drive for Pizza.....................................87

Festa della Republica (June 1st)....................89

More Haiku Six.......................................91

The body is home from Italy........................92

Part Two: Jacques en France

Tour Eiffel...97

Saint-Chappelle.......................................98

Rooftops of Paris.....................................99

Paris Visite (below the street)......................100

Momartre (Life Sustenance).......................101

Centre Georges Pompidou.........................102

First Tango in Paris.................................104

Part Three: Jakob in Deutschland

Mercedes Benz Bus 214 (Steinbach to Baden-
    Baden)...107

Approaching *Neuschwanstein*......................110

Europa Park 2013 (On the Spanish Benches)....111

Hauptbahnhof: Leaving Germany 2009.........108

Parts of Speech: In Germany 2011

Am Leopoldplatz im Baden-Baden.....................*114*

In der Konzertmuschel im Kurhausgarten...............*115*

Freiburg 07072011..................................... *116*

Beim Restaurant "Amadeus" im Leopoldsplatz..........*118*

In der Ev. Stadtskirche Baden-Baden..................*120*

In der Ev. Stadtskirche Baden-Baden....................*121*

Rastatt Residential Palace (Oldest Baroque
    Residence in the Upper Rhine Valley)...........123

Beim Gymnasium Hohenbaden......................….....*125*

Beim Matheunlerricht..................................*126*

Bei Herr Fesslers Musikunterricht.....................*128*

Politik..*129*

Physik..*130*

Bei den Baden-Badener Sommernächten.............…...*131*

Das Paradies 4..*132*

A la cathedral de Notre Dame Strassbourg..........*133*

Schloß Heidelberg.............................…......*134*

35. Internationales Oldtimer-Meeting...............*136*

Spitalkirche Orgelübung...........................*140*

Schülerkonzert mit Blockflöten In Klosterkirche

Poems From Travels In Three Countries

Lichtenthal..*141*

Orgelkonzert... *143*

Das Kurhaus.......................................*144*

Synagogue Site in Baden-Baden..............145

Basel am Montag Maulbronn Kloster (A U.N. World
Heritage Site) 147

*Alte Meister—Junge Solisten Baden-Badenen Philharmonie
Weinbrennersaal Kurhaus*...........................*152*

Orgelübung 6 Juli 2011.............................*153*

Europa Park 2011................................*154*

Lichtentaler Allee 16 Juli 2011....................*157*

*Museum Frieder Burda Bleckbäser des SWR
Sinfonicorchesters Baden-Baden and Freiburg*.....*158*

Am Marienplatz Juli 2011........................*160*

Riding to Salzburg.............................163

Salzburg.......................................165

Film "The Wave" *Die Welle*....................*166*

Deutche Bahn nach München........................*167*

At the Base Village of *Schloss Neuschwanstein*....*168*

Dachau Memorial Site...........................172

Schloss Nymphenburg..............................*174*

Final: Leaving *Deutschland*........................*175*

Türkische Mosque im Deutschland...................*176*

James R Ellerston

SWR Orckestra im Festspielhaus......................*177*

PART ONE

GIACOMO A ITALIA

WRITING

there are those of us

who struggle to organize

the words into lines and write poems,

as there are creative people

who like dancing through life

and strive to forge new styles

of ballet each day—

then fill the wide stage.

Italy was a time

I could not get the poems started

at the beginning of our trip,

(after our aborted flying experience);

travelers on our tour

suggested ideas and topics

from their own experiences;

my words and lines came in a flood.

Be On The Bus In The Morning

an endless cycle of hotels

long black tunnels, another tunnel

we blindly trusted Ferdinando

finding toilets without seats

travelling without luggage

room keys that weigh a pound

small hotel shampoos

being a vegetarian doesn't include chocolate

admission tickets for the toilet

the handicapped toilet is downstairs

Italian Birra

spaghetti, lasagna, fettuccini, penne

another Madonna and child under glass

fish with this, fish with that

red wine, white wine,

"the bus window reflects in my camera'

square bell towers in every town

marble this, and marble that

wait for the elevator or take the stairs

walking, walking on cobblestones

that tower leans

red Ferraris

wine, wine, and more wine

Limóncello, always great

25 toilets, 8 urinals, 3 hand driers, 1found toothbrush

watching out for cyclists

roses, roses, buy a rose, sunglasses, umbrella

stand and wait

meet under the watch and by the watch

ATM's for the daily limit

verdant hills

exact change for the toilet

"special discount for you"

admission ticket for this, for that

red poppies in the fields

434 steps to the top

wooden mattresses, paper-thin pillows

snow-capped mountains

email, Facebook, photos and friends

Lingua Italiana

the language of Italy

is one of food

and warm smiles,

cold *gelatos*

wine in glasses,

and coffee at the end of a meal

before *Limóncello* in small servings

to cap off the evening of conversation

after a dinner out or at home.

the drivers of cars

seem to know the ways of traffic

and weave their way between other autos;

those on cycles pulling through

with what seems mindless zeal,

and passing us on the highway

with what seems a death-wish—

making it back to safety in a lane

in the nick of time to stay alive.

everywhere one finds tourists

there are the hawkers from abroad,

holding their wares on dark-skinned arms

stretched out to interrupt your beer

while sitting *alfresco* in a *ristorante*

searching for a moments peace

between the admonishments of tour guides

to see damaged frescoes,

bell towers and crypts.

Deposizione Dalla Croce

the body of Christ

was taken down from the cross—

for humanity a redeeming loss;

his mother Mary held the corpse

draped across her arms;

Michelangelo saw her anguish

and in white marble carved her agony,

to be forever entombed behind glass

after the snap of a finger—

displayed for the rapid shutters of cell phones,

the gawking of tourists absent gazes—

for those without any understanding of the genius

captured in these marble faces

and muscles of a man tortured to death;

soldiers gambled for his garments;

the two are now forever shown in stony *Pietà* gaze;

while the ignorant gape and gossip

and move by in tour groups

anxious for their afternoon wine and dinner.

Coliseum: Photo and Song

I.

the Italian wears a shirt in the Coliseum

that simply says 'Kurt' with a picture—

as if we are supposed to know who and what;

in the sidewalk *ristorante*

Mother Mary speaks constantly

as Paul sings out that we should "let it be",

and it is more effective.

II.

If we were waiting

in line for the Parthenon—

the line would be straight.

III.

I do not hear lions,

I hear only grumbling;

when we had the ancient Romans

the entrance was free for the Christians

and they could see the lions for free—

their tragic exit came soon after.

Equestrian Salvation

when I could walk back to it,

at the bookstore I bought a horse

of cast bronze;

its form caught my eye,

but I let it go by,

later going back to the shop

and held out my card

to pay the clerk.

the skin is aged to a green patina

and cast with scripts;

I held it throughout the day with care,

while the sun sank down

and Forum stones did not hold my mind

for even one hour more.

I took it home

on the train in the ground

to rest on a shelf

in my room by my bed—

the sun will shine on it

each day when I wake from sleep

and dream of *Roma*,

in a place of great care

until I die;

I will have a long bare-back ride

clutching the mane for God,

like the Church told me to.

Pisa

White marble aches

do not climb as high as Jack's beanstalk,

but the tower leans in a graceful bow

for each visitor inclined

to clutch a plastic resin replica;

souvenir saledmen sell "Rolexes" from a tray for E20,

(they operate long enough

for us to drive away on the tour coach);

we resist all this in a churchyard

where one just gapes

at an engineering oddity gone bad,

while Italy struggles

to keep the tower from falling

with the certainty of its next government.

Child Workouts

we followed the Florence guide through

the *Galleria degli Uffizi* staring at paintings,

repeated subjects of Madonna and child—

Mary and *magi* depicted in eloquence,

sometimes a fragile child with wistful look,

other times a muscled child with formed arms;

(carpentry workouts with Joseph must have started early);

timbered arms and legs were voluminous

in the folds of the motherly shrouds of a delicate Mary.

staring at these pumped-up visions of Jesus,

we saw no grown teen in the temple but a child;

we spent the afternoon in religious contemplation,

but we never saw a vision of the final banquet;

we were excused from time for the *Galleria di Medici*

stretching across the river in the upper rooms.

Po Valley

an endless flatland of crops thirsting for moisture

while empty buildings wait for a watering of prosperity

in a land of larger fields, isolation, and recession.

wind breaks like silent sentinels in rows remind one

of the Red River Valley of the North in Minnesota;

pumps spray irrigation fountains under near cloudless skies.

our tour group has begun to long for home;

I am not interested in anything

except more mountains.

No Separation of Church and State in *Milano*

outside white marble spires reach skyward by the thousands,

but the inside is dark stone;

each capital is decorated with a level of statues,

but the most striking feature is military soldiers

guarding the entrance from hostile entrants,

wearing army green camouflage,

no attempt made to blend into the white stonework—

yet having the strength of the great bronze doors

to keep out the unwelcome.

Baveno on Lago Maggiore

water taxis lay at their moorings;

no early morning customers were at the breakfast buffets

while morning breezes swept across the water

seen through vertical acres of plate glass.

a man on a bench sat facing away from the lake,

avoiding the sun's glare across the length of the water;

bird song was stifled by the morning's jackhammer,

a mechanical iron woodpecker assaulting the ears.

sunlight lit the pink and yellow hillside villas

as I languished as a hotel guest up on my balcony;

a solitary gull glided the sky before my eyes

in the luxurious view toward the island restaurant.

an evening before, *Chianti* wet the lips

in tables of camaraderie of new-found friends;

columns of shrubs guarded ranks of vacant tables,

empty from night's revelry and wedding guests.

eyes were dizzy after the evening *Limóncello*,

livers saturated and anxiety dulled,

the mind cried out for morning caffeine

to make life bearable as the bus roared to life.

Monte Tamaro Svizzera (1961 m)

strands of steel transported

our gently rocking car of foursome

over the stiff towers

to the top wheel turning the car loaded cable,

depositing us out in an alpine meadow

of white crocus and melting snow packs.

we took off for the top of the hill

walking on soft grass and sliding on ice;

we both fell—

hands plunged into freezing frost—

the Aussie went down on his back;

I knelt down on one knee.

the next day bodies paid for our tumbles

as we were entrapped on the bus

within the lines of the freeway,

wedged in our stationary seat for hours—

fun exertion on the melting snow

had made for sound sleep later.

Verona

"Where for art thou"—

as we followed a tour guide

past walls, ramparts, and churches;

at last to the house of Romeo—

the young Montague;

and later the balcony of Juliet's "yonder pale light" –

as she leaned over the balustrade

poetically calling out for her Romeo;

(the breasts of her statuesque bronze body

undergo a constant adolescent polishing massage)

"Where for art thou"—

Pia counting bus passengers

coming late from *alfresco* lunches.

Verona: the Houses of Juliet and Romeo

there yonder the balcony of Juliet—

where a simple moonbeam on golden hair

set the heart of Romeo in cadence

until the morning crow of the cock,

and created a love story across the ages

ending in such despair,

despite the friar,

that the beating of two lovers' hearts

was deadly silenced;

later poets did scribe

and readers did anguish

such tragic misunderstanding

between Capulet's and Montague's

for centuries onward.

Venezia

(left behind in a tourist city)

we no longer can trust our tour guide

to watch out for us in a strange city;

Pia left our Adelaide friends behind—

"fend for yourself, find a train, bus, taxi,

to a hotel in the middle of nowhere",

(where farm fields stretched the eye to the horizon,

far from any city or even suburban centre).

Venezia itself, a gem of antiquity on the Adriatic coast

with its pastel domes and bell towers reaching skyward,

expands the past to the present

with older houses on narrow streets

leading to open *piazza*;

narrow alleyways end in bridges over canals

filled with murky waters and *gondolas*.

we walk the esplanade climbing one canal bridge after another;

brokers sell paintings, watercolors, t-shirts;

Poems From Travels In Three Countries

"three for Euro-twenty-five", (I bought three);

Chièsa San Marco is covered in scaffolding

and does not have the grandeur of the etching

in the musical history of Donald Jay Grout

(viewed four decades earlier with college innocence).

San Marco is but a mass of inlaid stone and mosaics

between the falling plaster of frescoes;

the boat ride on the salt-water lagoon,

on navigation paths marked with timber pilings,

takes us to an island of *Burano* filled with brighter colors,

a slower life, but still an avenue for tourists.

on *Burano* many of the wares were quality lace and linens;

a bottle of *frizzante* water satisfies thirst on our boat ride back to the
pier,

picking up most of our co-travelers

(leaving our Aussie friends waiting righteously by the clock

because of our early docking on the island and departure for reality);

re-docking the boat in the queue , could have replaced circling on the
bus.

we return to the salt flats,

where a life depends on fishing,

and cranes of shipping scrape blue skies,

the land turns to gardens in brown soil,

and the absence of sea-water canals

fingering between the fields going inland.

Ravenna (The Souvenir)

after the famed mosaic mausoleum, neck-aching views

of the ceilings of *Mausoleo di Galla Placidia,*

and time to hurriedly walk back to the bus,

we both saw it—

she said "the plate with the blue rooster";

my eyes were on it at the same time;

I entered the shop, and pulled the ceramic from display.

five layers of paper,

two of bubble-wrap, tape,

a paper bag and a plastic sack—

she made change for my fourteen Euro purchase;

walking down the street I commented,

"choosing the same souvenir, you can tell we are married";

(the cobblestones are difficult for both of us).

Ravenna (Caffè Farini)

on the corner of *Via De Roma and via Armando Diaz*

I see an Italian girl passing out cigarettes

to her friends sitting on the bench;

she smokes two;

she wears a T-shirt emblazoned 'Kurt Cobain 1967-1994';

she speaks rapid Italian with her mouth and her hands;

her eyes flick with thought;

black tennis shoes and *Adidas* shorts completed her outfit;

red hair is drawn up in a pony-tale atop her head.

the attraction of the music of Kurt Cobain to the world's youth

has survived now twenty years

after his untimely suicidal or brutally murdered death;

I do know that music and poetry which voiced

the 'smell of teen spirit' of a generation of adolescents

was worth teaching then and now;

it was not a mistake worthy of persecution;

a repetitive defiant voice still shouts out inside me,

"get on the bus, or miss the ride".

Umbria

Factories line the roadside,

Each with a long impressive name;

We can hardly catch them as past they slide;

Most in the USA lack any sort of fame.

Mile after mile they line our roadside view,

There aren't just one or few, but quite a dulling stream;

Flying past my window while I catch a snooze or two;

This barren sight of Italy was not my ideal dream.

The green hills of *Umbria* by our windows glide,

We could see the towns and towers atop their many slopes;

I sleep, not willingly, but from my closed eyes they hide;

My effort to enjoy, but a sleepy tourist copes.

Poppies line the roadsides in red or orange hue,

They remind us, saddened, of Flanders's distant fields;

Around each curve or tunnel exit springing into view;

We hear familiar lines a poet's pen painfully yields.

But poppies add a bright touch of much needed color

To a landscape of growing greens or fading arid browns;

Cameras point and people sigh at an Italian village's tower;

As poppies line the roadsides in red or orange gowns.

Under the Umbrian Sun

I see an ancient stone structure

    perched on a tree-covered hill,

I wonder about what kind of life I'd live there

    and whether anyone lives in it still.

I pick and choose as we drive by

    and point out ones where hill meets sky,

As if my life at home I'd change

    and with easy money move to Italy on the fly.

If my heart was really here

    amongst long meals with *prosciutto*, cheese, and wine,

Would I enjoy a shepherd's life

    of sheep-rung bells, or tending grapes upon the vine!

But come old age, the tempting house of rustic stone

    that seems around every curve to appear,

Would lose its attraction to an old gnarled cripple

    wishing for ancient birth-home held dear.

Yet if I found a palatial home I considered a find

    with it bought and mortgage signed,

I would hope to find a central peace of mind

    without rushing to work amid daily grind.

While if I could find the peace of Assisi

    under the Umbrian sun,

One could look out windows anywhere—

    indifferent to traffic, chaos, and work needing done.

Valley Highway View of Monte Cassino

The abbey of *Monte Cassino* sits white up on the hill

Commanding the valley from a strategic point yet still,

Guarding monks and valley as in days of yore;

The Abbey is new now after the Second War—

Bombs and attacks flattening buildings saved lives and cruel
wounded gore.

Today we pass so peacefully by motor coach on multiple lanes;

Just a passing look and distant photo mark regard for soldiers' pains;

Our guide says nothing and many sleep as we casually pass on by;

As the walls of *Monte Cassino* in the past fell to bombers on the fly—

So the present monks of *Monte Cassino* can now pray until they die.

Pompeii

These stones of antiquity tell a tale

Of falling ash and rock swept in a gale;

Of lives of old better than language now dead—

Their Latin words for scholars survived instead.

Volcanic destruction darkened the sky

While poisonous gasses called people to die;

A beautiful mosaic floor became a final bed—

While a time capsule was created for distant times ahead.

These paths of hurried Roman city life

Did not pass from existence by common warring strife;

Bodies of men, women, children preserved in stone—

Members of frightened families died quickly, often alone.

Archeologists dug layers of ash, soot and once molten rock

Finding an amazing site and a way to turn back the clock;

Today we walk these streets of *Pompeii's* vitality—

In amazement, that all this was preserved by fiery reality.

Seggiovia Monte Solaro (Anacapri)

I.

"You can always take the stairs down";

"If they could only make it all down hill";

But remember this—

Cecil B. DeMille did not make this movie,

and the hills and valleys could not be made *'plaine'*;

We have to trust the rail—

it is a bit abrupt isn't it;

"I'm a bit happier when I step back from that;"

(the birds circle below us in endless glides);

When you stare off the edge

the water is the deepest blue

(but there are no divers from Acapulco here).

II.

the sea air blows strong,

bringing up the sound of bells;

I eat a divine Magnum ice cream near the edge,

sucking the vanilla bar,

chocolate and almonds flaking off,

falling to the floor;

wind whistles in the pines;

tower pulleys on the cable car call out like gulls in flight

as we glide into people's gardens;

the cable rumbles from the strain;

a rooster crows to announce a scenic photo stop—

as Sorrento is entirely out of view in the cloudy haze;

it is not really raining,

the sky is merely sweating;

we look forward to a dessert of *Limóncello*

as the ferry heads into port.

Axel Munthe and *Villa San Michele*

This house, a small part of Sweden

    in which we were privileged to step,

Is full of artistic collector curiosities of Axel Munthe,

    antiquities and art

In a stone garden of rambling architecture

    which he himself found so brightly illuminated—

Where the sunlight shone too strongly

    for his declining troubling eyesight.

In later life he no longer lived in the villa itself,

    and hid his life away in a darkened tower,

Where he enjoyed solitude, the *Torre di Materita;*

    but even there in the darkness on Capri

Brilliance shown from his enlightened mind

    as a doctor and writer—

And secret lover of the Swedish Queen Victoria

    for thirty-two years and at her deathbed.

Circumnavigation of the *Isola di Capri*

steep rocky cliffs,

sea caves of coral,

stairs descend the cliffs for swimming;

("if the skipper keeps grinding the transmission

we will be lucky to get all the way around the island");

the sea is an incredible turquoise at the base of the cliffs

amid rock formations with fanciful names.

small white boats with sheltering sun canvas

swarm the sought-out cave entrances;

incredible pinnacles stretch out of the sea,

arches worn by sea water pierce the rock;

villas climb green valleys between the cliffs reaching the sea

or span saddles between the tops of the shorter valleys;

yachts anchor offshore.

the retaining walls of the highway snake the side of the rock

like a Great Wall leading pathways to other island towns;

the boat rides the slight swells;

gulls swim the surface to pluck their next meal from the waters;

Poems From Travels In Three Countries

it is high tide; at lower tide sea arches lead to inner grottos

sheltered from the sea, private worlds of color with names—

Grotta Verde, Grotta Azzurra, and *Grotta Bianca.*

green plants spring to life on steep walls

as we round the island attacking the waves of the open water,

bow rising and falling, buffeting the energy of the sea;

white villas perch atop the verdant cliffs;

the boat now pitches and rolls

as we round the end of the *isola*

the skipper slows the engines and rounds a mark.

my wife tries to find her sea legs.

as she gropes her way to an open window

gripping seat backs with each step;

one hand holds the camera

while another hand grips the boat—

to find a hand for the shutter is the challenge;

a white yacht cruises our port side;

a sand beach blends a row of swim cabanas

in peril from forceful waves.

a breakwater marks *Marina Grande*

as a deckhand puts dock fenders over the side

and sweeps spray from the deck;

the engines drop their reassuring revolutions

and we are tied up to life once again;

Capri is not a reality for tourists

but something magical and unattainable.

Moving Forward with the Crowd

thousands of fingers carved rivers

into the rough stones;

we are in a mindless sea of people

following the person ahead blindly,

hugging the rock wall,

stumbling from side to side as we are jostled;

a man commands harshly to move aside;

we are moving forward dumb without thought,

blindly following the crowd,

walking the slope with its two rails,

minding our steps from falling—

searching for our place

within the mass of sweating bodies.

it could have been the ramp

and the grapple for a place—

the endless scratching for cool air,

small children crying out today and then

in mothers' sheltering arms;

then people were silent, desperate;

today people talk loudly,

and push for a place in the line.

I am able to talk to my wife next to me,

calling out with dignity briefly above the din;

the diesel engine idles outside, coughs and shudders,

then roars into life—

and its fumes do not enter this safe-haven;

we are on the ferry from *Marina Grande* to *Sorrento*

crossing this choppy distance into another day of life,

even though today's sky is gray and overcast,

threatening rain on this sea of tired humanity

as we leave *Capri* for the rest of our lives.

*Written on a ticket for the 16:20 Capri-Sorrento ferry

Leaving Sorrento Behind

Two pines stand sentinel over biers of roses

as bags are packed and we have boarded our bus;

(one traveler stands alone having a last cigarette

     as if sentenced to be tied blindfolded to a post);

It is a climb down from the hotel by twisting paths—

Brave coach-drivers approach each other

     and weave their outside mirrors past each other,

as if driving a wide farm implement

     through a narrow farm field gate.

The island of Capri fills the bus windows

     as we descend toward the sea;

The sky fills with lifting morning haze;

Motor-cyclists surge past,

     weaving down a third center lane

(as if their helmet was the protective hand of a Roman god

     protecting them from burial in volcanic dust).

Direction signs point "*Napoli*";

    As we make another sharp corner, I gaze,

"Do I really want to come to Italy for an Irish pub—

    a *Guinness* instead of a *Peroni* draught?"

Our bus scrapes the center line through the city-centre

    as cars and cyclists push the extremities of their lanes;

Mother Theresa holds the *magi* with Mary,

    frozen in painted-tiles on the outside of a small church;

Our driver hops out for a smoke

    and to check the clearance for the bus on a center post.

There is a bed and breakfast pointed out by a sign—

(if this was our air-flight we would be staying overnight

    until they found a new bus that was maintained,

    and a driver who could work on the clock.)

We park at a rendezvous;

our smoker, who had a reprieve in his past,

    now smokes another cigarette in front of the wall,

    while the diesel rolls a drum cadence

    and cars fire past without command;

Our other troops arrive by a small bus—

    they all have green faces,

and stagger aboard our transport,

    after a baptism above the beach

    battling their way on coastal roads;

They ride as if blinded with eyes closed

    and seats gripped tight,

(they had been in a fight to include just one more town

    on their Italian tour);

We climb the cliff side,

    winding our way above the blue waters of the bay.

Murphy's Law dictates a Scottish pub here in Italy—

    fortunately we do not stop;

Packs of motorcyclists attack the side of the bus—

    none bites our flank;

Another tunnel opens on a commanding view of the sea,

    and an inviting but rocky beach;

It is morning still, and the sheltering umbrellas

    favor few bathers, are still closed tight from the night,

    and wait in regimental rows,

    marking territory in the sand;

We have conquered the expressway surf;

Through a strategic tunnel we leave the coastal highway behind

emerging on a viaduct

like the Milwaukee Skyway above the city,

until we are grounded between the sound barriers;

Reality looms—

an expressway marked "*Roma*".

on the way to *Roma*

we enter the expressway again,

signs point to *Napoli*;

factories and flats fly furiously past our window;

laundry dries on railings and lines off balconies;

on another the garden backs right onto the highway;

a cyclist roars by, "I don't care if I die, I am beating that bus,"

one hears the rasp of a future grave being dug;

red poppies already grace a highway ramp.

the bay is on our left,

cargo ships lie at anchor offshore;

we avoid local exits to *Napoli*

and choose the three lanes marked *Roma*;

the bus rolls by the *Via Appia*;

parallel rows of umbrella pines with narrow gravel between

claw through urban sprawl toward the horizon.

stone houses reach out to our restorative eye,

but are left abandoned by six lanes of the noise of diesel engines;

we fight our way up the valley— so easy now

without a hostile fascist army controlling the slopes and peaks;

our coach cruises the valley north;

waves in the asphalt provide a gentle rocking

which lulls my wife into sleeping away the miles

of green trees and concrete sound barriers;

our stomachs grumble as we wait for the Italian concept

of a lunch time in the afternoon at an AutoGrill—

and I have *penne* and *pesto* which was "al chewy".

we enter *Roma* with driving reminiscent of Minneapolis,

trucks weaving from lane to lane, then exiting within the mile;

a mixture of farm fields is along the highway,

with cranes scratching the sky above blocs of flats;

we pass the hotel jungle near *Fiumicino Aeroport*,

electrical transmission lines clouding the horizon.

Rome by Night

light and shadows,

monuments and fountains

leap into view with brilliant glory.

cool white cherubs and nude maidens

challenge the sensibilities,

while torsos of the naked Greek idea of manhood

with muscled bodies and an occasional spear

guard the waters splashing in the evening light.

the great dome of the Basilica St. Peter floats

above the city in its electric moonlight;

the *piazza* is empty enough to permit our tour bus

as shutters flash at the moving haze of Bernini's statues,

and our coach slowly drives around the colonnade.

eternal flames mark the tomb of the unknown soldier,

the "wedding cake" glorifies the struggle of armed conflict

before man starts it once again—

the two too-small flames, gasping for gas,

hardly compete with the glare of sodium and halogen

in the lights playing across the monument;

we see the balcony where Mussolini roused the crowds

to pitched heights of conquest for a modern Italian pride.

glaring signs for *Pizzeria, Hotel, Ristorante*

illuminate walks and gardens—

the desolation of city life for the 'down and out';

these are the haunts of young lovers,

bums with a bottle,

groups of walking young men talking,

and tourists seeking a taxi to a temporary hotel home.

there is always the roar of scooters;

girls sit on the rear seat with arms encircling the boy,

driving in a close embrace

as the machines shift through the 'hick-ups' of several gears,

buzzing like dragon-flies away into the night.

impending darkness has an uncertainty,

does not embrace us in a welcoming velvet purple horizon;

it is a play of grayness, of solitary isolation,

is a cauldron of red auto lights braking at traffic signals,

and of halting goodbyes between strangers.

sharp evening shadows fill the urban forest;

the *piazza*s are filled with foreign hawkers—

always the prints, the leather, the toys, the roses;

musicians sing to finance their pitiful impoverished futures—

we move into ours at the end of our journey together.

Five *Haikus*

In *Roma*

The Saint Peter's church

stands imposing white *a Roma*

to reach nearer God.

Pietà vaticana

Crowds saw Mary's tears

as their own slid down faces

at Christ draped in death.

A Purchase

I bought a painting

of sailboats on the beach in

a Sorrento dream.

Lost Luggage

One finds how little

one really has need of

without one's lost bags.

Not Dry

I sought a picture

of gondolas in Venice

canals dark and wet.

tour's end

morning hoots of owls,

songs of birds;

shadows warm to sunshine

and smiles of farewells;

Ferdinando has driven

our hectic travels;

Pia has guided our journey;

now Italy feels like our own country.

apartment in the *Roma* sky

we are welcomed to the apartment in the *Roma* sky;

kisses and hugs greet us as if we were already family;

the younger son translates our meanings for his mother;

we are offered beer and wine, the food,

and now the *mandarino*;

art prints, paintings and pottery grace the living space;

the bed sleeps well for our *siesta*;

Alessandro will sing choruses in *La Boehme* tonight—

he will be at the theatre soon—

we will miss him in the evening family circle;

we see photos of a future son-in-law

as a child at the seashore with his younger brother;

there is an early Roman pottery *amphora*

and a parrot of *Murano* glass

next to a napping Papa on the divan;

traffic sounds of cycles, cars, and low-pitched trucks

mingle with the sounds of children

in the tree-filled green-space below;

they call-out to each other at play;

a distant radio serenades an afternoon glass of *Peroni;*

through open doors to the balcony

where afternoon laundry grazes under a sinking sun;

Papa snores on

and seashells speak the ocean without syntax or pause.

apartment life 2

we napped away the afternoon

after our meal of pasta and seafood;

wine as always with an Italian meal;

fish was purchased fresh this morning

out of the many stalls at the market—

different fish in foam shipping boxes

in the large concrete building;

we walked-about sampling cherries and apricots

for flavor and texture;

our arms grew heavy as various bags

accumulated on one arm,

the other kept free to sample fruit and point;

strawberries and melons filled more bags;

there were shrimp and mussels

for today's and tomorrow's meals.

meals were over a bright orange tablecloth

with joyous laughter,

grammar discussions of Italian and English, conversation and wine.

Haiku *a Roma*

Dusk

Roman sky at twilight—

glowing clouds move in
circles,

cool breezes blow.

Appiana Antica

Driving cars on the Appian
Way—

is off-roading,

on Roman stones.

Roma

Urban war—

loud ambulance sirens sound,

wounded are hurried away.

Lugano

A meeting time by the lake—

where new autos were
displayed,

with closed stores.

Amphora

A Roman antique—

old jar cast into the sea,

enriches daily life.

Boat to *Burano*

Piles pounded in the lagoon—

guided our boat safely there,

to see linens.

More Haiku Two

Breakfast

the melon ripens in the sun

as do close family ties

at meals.

Impressionism

the sun on buildings by the sea

glows on pastel house and
church

and boats.

Signora

she sweeps the apartment
floor

hurrying to the kitchen

to start our meal.

Opera

Alessandro sings at the
Opera—

we do not see him

on stage.

In Awe

we wait for the car

to see the Coliseum—

an ancient building.

Geographica

we study the maps

to see where we are going

and where we have been.

Even More Haiku Three

Commander in Chief

a man in blue

has studied with Obama

so he waves his finger.

Class System

all seats are taken;

the old women have vinyl
bags—

tourists buy leather.

Michelangelo *La Pietà*

in Saint Peter's Church

Mary cradles the white marble
Christ

deceased in her arms.

Tourist Photos

always the scaffolding

repairing old monuments

for future times.

Cups and Glasses

in Italy

both the coffee and liqueurs are
strong

and both have little servings.

Subway Station

a river of people flows

up the subway escalator

to change trains.

Backyard

I sit on my deck of tile

held high in the sky *a Roma*

filled with the blooms

that are watered daily

with love and care—

to make one's time at home

filled with more joy at life;

I drink my beer

at the end of each day

and sit in the shade

from the sun—

while the *signora* cooks the food

on the hot gas stove

and we are served

a good meal

on the bright cloth,

and drink wine with friends

who will be forever

loved as family

Museo di Montecassiono

the abbey looms high on the mountain,

reached only by a winding road,

a series of switchbacks looking out

across the valley green.

between abrupt corners

a curving stone wall keeps us in our place;

we reach the top along with a tourist bus—

a group of noisy middle-schoolers from *Napoli*.

the students chatter and chide loudly

but next to the nave of the church,

gazing at the altar rebuilt after the second war,

they are silenced by the attendant.

we and the students are hurried out for a mass;

we choose the abbey museum

and are immersed in the art, artifacts,

and splendor of high church.

once bombed into oblivion

by Allied forces February 15, 1944,

so much of a thousand-year history was blown away

to be rebuilt for the monks of the order.

Monte Cassino has risen again—

a phoenix of white stone and quiet peaceful fountains,

still looking out over the critical road to *Roma*;

a lot is here for our attentive tourist eyes.

Italian Meal in a Farm Home

we had an Italian meal last evening

with an Italian extended family;

our attentive Roman host visited his "milk-mother"

(the woman who raised him from twenty days to five years of age,

before he returned to the care of his birth mother—

she enrolling him in a collegium);

his attachment was for the "milk-mother"

who had nursed his early life.

we were in a dining room in a house on a hill;

ten chairs were around the long table,

laden with sausage, *prosciutto*, bread and wine;

a chicken and pickled bean plate

was followed by cooked greens, omelet,

and more wine in our emptied glasses;

there were ten persons around the table;

(the host Papa sat next to me.)

our meal concluded with liqueur,

a strange mix of alcohol and herbs;

the taste was pungent;

our host presented me with a bottle

for evenings at home in the States;

honored, I was invited to return to teach English;

I would like to learn the language

and also learn to make pizza in a wood-fired oven;

there was much conversation in Italian;

the plastic-manufacturing family

also does business in America.

as a tourist it was a wonder to visit a family home

with a great-grandmother living out her life

in her cottage down the hill,

and a child at play in the yard—

ignoring the cats;

I could speak the language

of stroking and scratching the dog,

but he only responded to commands in his native tongue;

I could only speak Italian with my hands;

Massimo knew the German word *Nein*

and enriched the dog's life to be bi-lingual.

At the House of *Renato Valeri*

Via Campo Isabella

We sit around a table for ten,

an extended family did descend;

and great-great-grandmother who raised *Massimo*

and is long-time loved and praised.

We eat the farm-cut chicken,

children and grandchildren together;

the great-great grandchild *Thomas*

dances his request for our attention.

A good time was had by all,

for our visit the family was glad;

Massimo lived here long ago;

He still visits the family he enjoyed today.

Renato gave me a bottle of "bitters",

to drink on a winter night; at their house

I was invited to teach English, again

if I have the courage to take another flight.

We enjoyed hospitality into the night,

with hugs and kisses as if long-time friends;

a meal with an Italian family around a table

had been a dream— now no longer a distant fable.

Even More Haiku from Italy Four

E45 Highway

The road stretches to Naples;

we follow its dotted lines

home in peace.

Italian News Broadcast

We are smiling people

even when reporting news

that is tragic.

Tiananmen Square at 25 Years

One student was unafraid--

stopping an armored tank gun

for the world.

Communications

Dictionaries during meals

translate words we want to say

with meaning.

Fiery Ride

Fire engines sound their sirens;

some one has a blazing good ride

in Rome.

Mediterranean Sea in *Anzio*

Such straight lines

the horizon draws against

a blue sea in Anzio.

a parody of the poet John Keats

a thing of humor is a laugh forever;

its funniness increases;

it will never pass into pensiveness,

but still will make a friend laugh with us

on a day full of remembered jokes

and good health,

and quiet chuckling to one's self.

*after visiting the house of Keats

one of Fagin's boys

today, on my ninth trip to Europe

I lost my wallet;

I paid one Euro at the *Farmacia*

and did not pay attention

as I crushed onto a city bus

and pushed my way into a subway car.

while riding, my heart sank

at my empty pocket;

I felt I had been unguarded

and also become a victim—

but neither have we fallen,

have not been hurt;

(except for a badly bruised elbow),

have not been sick.

Having one's person violated by theft

makes one feel alone—

even with wonderful hosts

who helped to ease the pain;

but I awakened in the night with anger,

and in the morning was reluctant

to face the day;

I have warned so many students,

and have succumbed myself.

in the long run, the thief gets one's money

or the government taxes it away.

three coins in the fountain

we visited fountains *a Roma,*

where the play of the water

made one feel like children;

people crawled like ants to take pictures,

of the old fountains with cameras,

cell phones, and today's tablets;

but we sat on benches like the old

and warmed,

soaking in the afternoon sun.

James R Ellerston

fruit farm visit

on a narrow road between bearing trees

we visited the farm of fresh fruit

and tasted washed peaches;

our host *signora* made her choices;

we enjoyed the samples, spitting pits,

and drove the car between the trees

on an abundant pathway.

going home, on the government form

we will check "we have not visited a farm";

there were no animals, but three pet dogs and a cat,

but our answer is far from the truth

of our gracious visit amongst the orchards,

where I was served "Naples coffee"

in a small glass by the owner,

between eating apricots.

Sicily-Rome American Cemetery and Memorial

from the *Tyrrhenian Sea*

the troops came ashore in waves

at the *Anzio/Nettuna* landings

under the rain of bullets

the twenty-second of January 1944;

many veteran soldiers were lost

new draftees died;

some bodies were found,

some missing in battle.

now ranks of crosses and Jewish stars march

in battle-hardened rows across the lawns

of the cemetery, to remember those

who crossed the beaches under fire

almost seventy years ago

to free Italians from fascist rulers,

and those who would make war in Europe.

in the sacred chapel are names

of those whose bodies were never found;

outside are rows of unnamed white marble

marking the honored bodies of the unknown;

while rows are curved to the eye—

the buried of a noble fight for freedom

went straight to God's salute;

today their remains pass sun-filled afternoons

in their eternal bed in Italy under the American flag;

in bright daylight, a nearby reflecting pool bleeds red

to mourners' eyes.

Even More Haiku 5

After the Thief

It is funny traveling

with no cards, no money,

no wallet.

Roman Sport

Boys in parks play basketball;

even green pine trees in cars

smell of "Sport".

Michelangelo

A genius sees David

in a block of white marble

carving stone.

Sunday Bells

Church bells of *Roma* ring out,

tolling sounds across cities

on Sunday.

One's Work

It is good to have a day job

if you have a poet's muse

to write.

Galleria Borghese a Roma

we visited the sculptures;

the marble boy sits hunched in the corner,

innocent, adolescent, nude, white-skinned,

working at the splinter in his foot

with a curved needle—

such honest reality in carved white stone.

the sculpture reminded me of a posture

the teen lifeguard has at the swimming pool;

he often sits with one leg crossed over,

wide-shouldered, bent, muscled, working-away

at his left foot while sitting in the guard chair—

beautiful, unselfconscious in young manhood.

we saw a sculpture looking like my child;

her stony face so resembles

my daughter's attitude when she is upset;

the maiden erotically lies on her side,

and her vision commands the space—

a room full of museum goers on a Sunday afternoon.

my daughter lies curved on the couch

snuggled next to a small loving dog;

though the comedy plays-out on television

her eyes have a far-away attitude;

her pale lips are pursed when she thinks of work—

cooling the hardwood floor to marble cold.

a drive for pizza

in the evening

we drove twisting mountain roads above the lake

and see *Lago Albano*,

where across the waters on the shore

the Pope also escapes the heat of *Roma*

for the deep waters of the collapsed volcano;

a cool breeze blew through the trees.

in the town of *Genzano*

we were in the *ristorante Il Tinellol*

for the pizza and beer;

afterward the evening was late;

we saw floral petal designs in the street

made by the children of the town

for the festival.

people celebrating the holiday weekend

were walking the streets at nearly midnight;

we only walked to find our parked car,

strolling among revelers and teen boys

all outdoors under tents at the *foosball* table games;

our driver *Alessandro* took the faster roads

home to the city— but they felt slower.

Festa della Republica **(June 1st)**

military jets fly over *Roma*

while people jam the bleachers

watching the parades—

the bands, flags, swords and weaponry;

dignataries rise and clap,

as military divisions march past

the television cameras showing

different uniforms, hats, and masks.

white horses trot

followed by brown and black in formations—

their backs strapped with timpani on each side,

cymbals and trumpets in uniformed hands.

for the anthem of Italy all rise,

while the horses stand at attention;

the President boards an open car

for a motorcade through the streets and crowds.

(they have not yet learned

from Archduke Francis Ferdinand in 1914,

or JFK in 1963, or the Holy Father in his pope-mobile

to have bullet-proof glass against revolutionaries).

meanwhile Italian naval forces

welcome refugees from Africa

who wish to be Italian to the EU,

from their desperate boats at sea.

immigrants sell handbags and scarves

to tourists in the cities in the *piazza*

and to *alfresco* diners at their tables,

showing an effort to fit into the economy.

planes fly the colors of Italy

from their contrail streams;

the crowd disperses, and the old guard

   of the government congratulates each other's power.

More Haiku 6

Sit-com

Television speaks Italian;

but lips do not move with the

speech.

San Pellegrino

Drink the sparkling water

direct from the mountain
springs;

bubbles rise up.

Red Poppies

In Italy red poppies grow,

not on graves but in fair fields

roadside.

On the Terrace

We hear the children at play,

at fun in the park below

all laughing.

A Country Meal

All of the family

lives together on one farm

at one table.

Poetry

I write of *Italia*,

a few words just scribbled
down

on paper.

the body is home from Italy

my mental doldrums are listless,

and are filled with golden sunlight on quay-side buildings,

wheat-straw fields yellow by the roadside

splashed with bright-red poppies growing wild,

grey-green olive trees marching in hillside groves,

rows of string-held grape vines

clinging to slopes in obedient rows.

it is the sea that caught my imagination in the spectrum;

whether the Bay of Naples or the Venetian Lagoon

or bright painted boats laying on tidal beaches,

(painted in bright oils on the rolled canvas I brought home),

tourists scurried

to the water-taxis' golden glistening varnish

for the thrill of sitting on wooden seats

riding under power across the lagoon.

murky green canals beneath white Venetian bridges

are veins and arteries of water penetrating the shadowy

flesh of crumbling island life

as old buildings sink slowly into the sea;

pastel-pink domes rise skyward across the lagoon

(a panorama of muted colors not seen elsewhere)

are printed on the mind

in streaks of watercolor memory indelible.

gray seas splashed

as one cruised under threatening clouds

around the villages and beaches of Capri,

an isolated paradise of huddled buildings

rising on the slopes

up from waters whose high tides

blocked our view of colorful ocean grotto caves

on our round-island cruise.

in *Villa San Michele* there was the grey-white marble

of rising columns and busts with broken noses

and intelligent piercing eye sockets

staring oneself down from centuries past;

(my bronze horse galloped home

from the Coliseum to my table);

dark brick-red ruins of the past glory that was Rome

rise from the excavated pits of archeologists

in mental ruins of past studied Latin.

amphitheaters lacked the inspiring oratorical wisdom

of a contemporary long-term senator

speaking of empire, power, and conquest;

(the stabbing pain of dormant arthritis

took over my hobbled journey through the Roman Forum);

it is colors and shadings that I brought home with me;

I now need sunlight to turn the northern lake waters blue

to match the daylight-sky outlined by deep-green trees,

and the passage of more time to feel at home here again.

PART TWO

Jacques en France

Poems From Travels In Three Countries

Tour Eiffel

Woven lattice-work of iron cast soaring skyward,

into gentle curve of arching strength,

a gliding mechanism of early technology elevating us

rising upward and higher to the topmost platform—

to see Paris like a banquet spread on linen white,

reaching horizons before us.

Strength of engineering imagination holds us

uplifted in riveted excellence;

an idea undefined by simple mathematics

but by the fertile mind of genius—

wheels turning, motors spinning,

and the elevator car rides the rails.

The finest of mere mortal thoughts

brings us closer to the heavens

this structure available to those a century earlier—

brought people ever closer to the mind of God—

easily available by reaching towering heights

now for us mere pocket change and a wait in line.

Saint-Chappelle

Curtains of gothic glass screen the idea of eternal home

    from our earthly plodding,

as if held heavenward by no mere construction of toiling man

    extending walls in art glass prism of sky-hewn blue,

fractions of vivid dyed pallet

    deep fabled colors in leaded patterns;

stories of the Bible in picture

    eleven-hundred times in pictured design

conveying fabled truths to masses of believers

    able understanding of portrayed dramas illustrated to the eye

in a time when spoken studied Latin text poured forth

    for the city dweller and peasants deaf but eager ears.

Rooftops of Paris

sheltering roofs with chimney pots;

the creation of deluxe apartments in the clouds;

rooftops doing battle against the sky-lighted heavens,

elevating the dimensions of the street upward,

outlining paths in climbing living space;

mere plants, the trees around flowered gardens become

amongst the throngs of ants below congregating

and marching in paraded cadence

beneath your endless mansard crown,

ever expanding in late afternoon light and shadow

beneath this viewer's eyes.

Paris *Visite* (below the streets)

below the streets the electric trains surge

rushing from one lighted stop to the next,

traversing distances of blackened tunnels

hurtling through tubes of concrete walls

under teeming lives of businesses, hotels and corporations,

three-piece-suits next to sandals and T-shirts,

conveying shopper, tourist and worker,

powered by the technology of electricity

strung on wires beneath acres of cavernous ceilings,

transporting man into the myriad activities of urban life.

Poems From Travels In Three Countries

Momartre (life sustenance)

smells of foods, scents of oil paints

vast tents of crowded tables, lines of artists' stalls and easels

menus selections offering in language, a parade of colorful patinas

choice of sustenance, eye grabbing designs

reading options *en Francais*, grasping a picture

desired by a needing soul

food for hunger, a satisfied vision

one plate served, one canvas designed

courteous service, care in packaging

quickly consumed nourishment, a future hanging for a wall

an afternoon which might be forgotten, eternal value in
choice

a chef's work in the kitchen, a painter's work in open air

seafood on a platter with sauce, paying for a sunny day and
location

the art of French cooking, an idea of oils on canvas

Momartre afternoon in memory forever, fishing boats at low
tide,

two moments' decisions, too much money for having both

happy after the meal, eyes feast on the sea in my inner space.

Centre Georges Pompidou

a proud warrior,

 stretched

  out in battle

   against the traffic

    racing forward in city streets.

wounded gut grasping soldier,

 shred of outer skin

  clasping bowels against his body

   as great tubes of life-bearing dynamic

    enter and exit this courageous battlefield.

displaying images digested by multitude thousands of once artistic
dead, .

 energized and intellectualized

  shown the food of soul and mind,

   who pass through miles of galleried veins and arteries,

    the heart and sustenance of expressive civilization.

required tourist spot searching out the wealth of Paris minds alive,

on our student journey a first day battle in the city

myriad subway connections bravely followed

to this easily accessible tomb of art

to architecture at its most recognizable.

First Tango in Paris

In the art gallery, on the subway, in the *Place de la Republic,*

within groups of tourists at *Cathedral Notre Dame,*

in *la café* for a spot at a table,

there is a constant stepping to the side,

an avoidance of others dancing their way down the street

on a concrete tango floor filled with hurried pedestrians

following the rhythm of the city, the music of daily-life—

a pulse controlled by manners, custom, and urgency.

We step rhythmically aside, under our breath mutter *excusez moi*

as we assertively claim our ballroom path and space

for steps in pattern in our sought-out direction;

this is not the slow-mourning tango of Argentina

(moaning the death of an Evita)

but the rapid Latin tango of a vital Paris day

filled with youthful energy and the quick-step

of those who know where they are going

or wish to go.

PART THREE

Jakob in Deutschland

Mercedes Benz Bus 214 (Steinbach to Baden-Baden)

The bus downshifts roughly again,

transmission whining

rounding ever twisting curves

with audible effort climbing the hills of the Black Forest

on the way to earned marks and chosen schools,

from villages now part of the merged city.

All ages ride this morning bus,

from the primary child

to the changed voices of male teens

always occupying the dominant rear postures of the bus,

hurling muscled words at each other

to overcome the engine's diesel roar beneath their seats.

Two adolescent girls wearing orthodontics are smiling

all the time at the blond boy's attention,

nodding heads while listening attentively;

again the bus downshifts and jerks again,

sloshes the passengers from side to side

with all-sized hands grabbing for stability.

The 214 bus is a major churning vessel to multiple schools

carrying young cargo to the *stadt-mitte*;

students hopping on at different stops along the road,

climbing bus steps lightly,

springing their way into seats

displaying or shadowing school-age personalities.

Each morning the same dance persists for seats—

a game of musical chairs with respect for those older,

mutual neutrality for classmates,

a balancing of stuffed heavy backpacks

and adolescents shifting from one foot to another

hanging from pipes and bars in their Nikes.

The ride is a time of conversation for some,

or greeting classmates and friends;

others sit in silence,

unaware of the body wedged against them,

dreaming, brooding, or in self-reflection,

through morning mist and cloud.

The bus downshifts again, transmission whining,

rounding another twisting curve— winding lives together;

adjacent perspiring bodies in humid tangent cling to solitude

finding no intersection of their circles of life,

with only guard-rails on the mountain roads

to protect private lives in enforced silence on a spiraling journey.

Approaching *Neuschwanstein*

mountains rise blue with forest growth

above flat land rushing to their heights;

houses slumber in their red tiled coverings

in the flat blankets of the uplands;

snow does not hide the towering peaks

these lingering evening beds of summer solstice—

rock outcroppings tower barren;

white castle walls poise above us

starkly outlined against striking slopes;

yellow flowers in a box on a window sill

add color to the scene of tree and stone

as our train rolls on through another day in *Bayern*.

Europa Park 2013 (On the Spanish Benches)

The red and yellow benches stand empty

under an awning tented from bright sun;

I wait alone in a silent world of departed souls,

where once castanets compelled great dancing:

swaying slender hips of dark-haired men

and rounded skirts of young women—

black leather stretched across the forest of fertility

from one curved hip to another

as cubist folds of sensual womanhood

merely brush-stroked by painter's imagination

were accentuated by flashing eyes and flirting bodies,

while the middle dancer pounded out beats

with his cane striking the floor faster and faster

until erupting clapping suddenly was coming forth

and rhythmic surging of the driven rod stopped breathlessly;

dancers panting in ecstasy of motion

now silenced and abruptly still.

Hauptbahnhof: Leaving Germany 2009

The speeding train hurdled across the south German countryside;

Cities and towns going rapidly past:

    one look-alike small station after another

    seen through the rain-streaked windows;

It was in Nuremberg I had seen them—

    the man holding the bulging backpack for the young girl

    as they gave each other a quick hug—

    while the father kissed the girl on the forehead;

Afterward he stood there on the brick-tiled platform

    staring at the side of the train

As she bounced with youthful confidence

    and professional poise down the aisle

    dropping into the seat across from me;

The father was giving a gentle wave with a wrinkled hand

    as he tried to peer through his own reflection

    in the gray shroud of sky caught on the glass;

She really did not see his timid wave

    as she settled herself in her seat

    and responded to my inquiry about where she was going:

Poems From Travels In Three Countries

"Los Angeles in America where she would meet friends

    from San Francisco and have a holiday;"

The train began slowly rolling;

    the father was left quickly behind;

And the train raced on through the overcast morning

    towards the airplanes and runways in Frankfurt.

It has been the same for ten thousand partings,

    a thousand times over;

Trains, platforms, the final whistle—

    then parental longing.

Only yesterday it had been almost the same—

    But that I was the gray haired man,

    And the mother of the children was my wife—

      a mother hugging the son she loved

      and kissing the daughter goodbye;

I was the father covered with the foul-scented perspiration (of nervous sweat)

      who was so easily pushed away by the anxious girl—

      and not invited into a last loving embrace;

So the warm lips of the father

so briefly touched the center of her perfumed forehead

and his palm brushed against her soft scented hair.

His son dashed up at the last minute—

from a food stand coming quick with sandwiches

within paper sacks between his outstretched hands—

And received his father's lips pressed against his gentle forehead too

(a kind of rite of passage like Ash Wednesday—

the placing of a mark onto the forehead

of those believing in a future—

usually at the beginning of a new period of time such as Lent);

But this was a time when the parents were giving up something—

the company of their children's daily lives—

so the children could move forward toward growth.

It has been the same for ten thousand partings,

a thousand times over;

Trains, platforms, the final whistle—

then parental longing.

The train began rolling and the father and mother

were left behind standing stiffly on the platform

under the noisy skylights in the central Munich station;

The mother wept and wiped her tears—

    tears of pain, parting, and also joy—

But brother and sister were now smoothly rolling

    through the sunshine of a southern journey;

(He the scholar of the German language about to study Italian,

    and she, the young singer of Puccini arias,

    off to sing her heart out in Italy);

This mother and father had stared at the train-car window

    as it had sat still on the track;

Seated across from each other at the table

    the brother and sister exchanged the looks

    of a pleasant banter of conversation;

The mirror of the train window projected the image of a tired man

    and an anxious but proud woman;

A departing train was visible through

    the parallel-universe windows of the car's other-side;

Another departing train was reflected

    upon the semi-opaque window nearer—

Multiple trains moving in industrial harmony

    against the American-Gothic pose of the man and wife—

    in counterpoint forming the surrealist stage-set

for this real-life drama.

It has been the same for ten thousand partings,

a thousand times over;

Trains, platforms, the final whistle—

then parental longing.

The father limped and favored first his right knee and then his left

as he took small stooped-over steps off the platform;

The mother, bracing herself to the upcoming length of the absence,

strode briskly ahead, poised and energetic;

Both had pained and drained faces—

but their fingers intertwined for a middle-aged instant—

a somber reality settling in:

Children have their own lives outside of the family.

This time I was the man on the platform,

and the woman struggling in tears was my wife;

she was the mother of my children;

This time my son and my daughter

were traveling together on the departing train;

This time it was a train headed for Milan

from Munich Hauptbahnhof.

It has been the same for ten thousand partings,

a thousand times over;

Trains, platforms, the final whistle—

then parental longing.

James R Ellerston

Parts of Speech: In Germany 2011

Am Leopoldplatz im Baden-Baden

Flags waving, fountains spraying, children playing;

Train-riders hurrying, parents worrying, waiters scurrying,

Chefs currying;

Shoppers spending, relationships mending, friendships tending;

Cyclists cranking, money-changers banking, jokesters pranking;

Busses grinding, schedules minding, mountain-roads winding;

Planes soaring, rains pouring, trucks roaring;

Wealth spreading, sandals treading,

Groom's and bride's wedding;

Arthritics' moaning, muscle-builders' toning,

butchers' deboning;

Bier-mugs foaming, tourists roaming, beauticians combing;

Cathedrals inspiring, athletes perspiring, the worn-out retiring;

Tree leaves rustling, hoarders bustling, sales-persons' hustling;

Old-folks hobbling, toddlers wobbling, repairmen cobbling.

Poems From Travels In Three Countries

In der Konzertmuschel im Kurhausgarten

Announcer hailing, saxophonist wailing, bassist flailing;

Barbeques grilling, water glasses spilling

Musicians' whistling, neck-napes bristling

Teen-agers necking, neighbors beckoning,

phone-lovers texting;

Band-shell audience shivering, vibrato quivering,

Dancers maneuvering;

Wine glasses tinkling, walked-dogs sprinkling,

dollar's-value shrinking;

Planes soaring, rains pouring, trucks roaring;

Swing-rhythms bouncing, pick-pockets pouncing,

Singers announcing

Flowers blooming, rock-bands booming, castles looming;

Fountains spraying, worried praying, flags waving.

Carousel spinning, friends grinning, gamesters winning.

James R Ellerston

Freiburg 07072011

Medieval cathedral stands defiantly;

Tall steeple soars skyward;

Dim candle lights dimly;

Careful bombing circumvents successfully;

Webbed scaffolding towers upward;

Electric elevator climbs daringly;

Clear water flows swiftly;

Good *Döner* cooks quickly;

Thin pizza bakes deliciously;

Red building survives singularly;

Tired students meet punctually;

Impatient teen talks rudely;

Tented stall tempts expensively;

Humorous lady leads happily;

Retired commentator entertains knowledgeably;

English guide speaks informingly;

Stone crypt drips horrifyingly;

Student shopper buys impulsively;

Threatening rain delays enough;

Fast train arrives promptly;

Green Party represents ecologically;

Colored window portrays vividly;

Craft guild advertises discreetly;

Much coin finances restoratively;

Mosaic streets paved smoothly;

Free time eaten eagerly;

Old houses rebuilt imitatively;

Inattentive travelers de-train hurriedly;

Fascinating *Großmütter* converses historically;

Golden *Bier* quenches satisfyingly.

James R Ellerston

Beim Restaurant "Amadeus" im Leopoldsplatz

I sit at my elevated table

up a few steps from the street;

The white umbrella protects me from the sun

and gives me a sense of security;

I watch people on the square below

as they hurry about their business

or wonder aimlessly with a dog

leading at their side;

Young teens gather in clusters

which are filled with laughter;

The old move about with canes and struggle

on and off the many city busses;

The clatter of the diesel bus engines

mixes with the music of street musicians.

We eat our meal and drink *Bier*,

all at a price we can afford in *Euro*,

and consider it a good value in dollars;

We do not order the dessert available here—

Poems From Travels In Three Countries

but save space for the ice cream specialty store

in the narrow alley up the street from *Deutche Bank*—

where we will replenish our cash

after replenishing our stomachs.

In der Ev. Stadtskirche Baden-Baden

Church bells pealing, conscience healing, converts kneeling;

Organist leading, young-people reading, congregation needing;

Proud-parents gushing, the marriage-unfaithful lushing,

youth-readers mushing;

Pastor preaching, soloists screeching, old-Catholics beading,

offering-gatherers pleading;

New-born Christening, audience listening, sun-rays glistening;

Believers confirming, confirmants affirming,

undecided-souls discerning, dying yearning,

condemned squirming, deceased worming.

Poems From Travels In Three Countries

In der Ev. Stadtskirche Baden-Baden

The crucified Christ hangs in painted glass above the altar;

The congregation scattered about in seats

arrived early for the service;

The organ waltzed forth with "Morning has Broken"

as sunlight streamed through the colors

of the nativity scene.

We gathered at the river for a Baptism;

The water was gently placed on the young teen's head—

She quickly brushed her hand through her hair from reflex;

Tea and cookies followed the Benediction

(To eat is the same in any language.)

But *mein Sohn* shepherds me beside the river *Oos*,

as swiftly flowing it plays over flat paving stones

laid in the bed of the river;

The young girl had just waded in,

and stood barefoot on a bottom stone,

next to the pastor in clerical robes

but also barefoot on simple stones.

The day was blest;

The rain held off;

There was only window shopping in Baden-Baden on *Sontag*.

Rastatt **Residential Palace**

(Oldest Baroque Residence in the *Upper Rhine Valley*)

Coral-colored walls, rock-climbed vines;

Green-watered lawns, stone-paved courtyards;

Pea-rocked paths, body-rotated statues;

Sun-blocked shadows, gold-gilded clocks;

Tall-scaffolded construction, idle-seated students;

Plastic-bagged purchases, costume-dressed actors;

Tree-arbored gardens, cool-wafted breezes;

Multi-paned casements, short-ticketed train-rides;

English-guided tours, fashion-imitated royalty;

Rapidly-walked parks, accurately-preserved chambers;

Romantic-errored paintings, agony-twisted sculptures;

Curling-plastered ceilings, jewel-bedecked coats;

Formal-"*Plié*" steps, defeat-portrayed Turks;

Recently-cleaned frescos, close-stitched tapestries;

High-curtained beds, wood parquet floors;

Faux-painted columns, blood-trapped fleas;

Oil-perfumed bodies, crystal-lighted chandeliers;

Ornate-mantled fireplaces, white-wigged courtiers;

Graceful-gowned girls, awkward-curtsied advisors;

Quickly-changed wigs, slowly-dresses Margrave;

Early-deceased ancestors, acting-adolescent imposters;

Soon-returned reality, past-faded memories.

Beim Gymnasium Hohenbaden

Knowledge seeking, highest-level peaking,

Really-smart geeking;

Phone-lovers texting, teen-agers beckoning,

Desk-neighbors beckoning;

Mistakes flagging, low-pants sagging, parents nagging;

School children testing, braggarts besting, teen-couples nesting;

Students learning, young-minds burning, stomachs churning,

(Headmaster's-looks sterning);

Teachers grading, failed-classes evading, blue-jeans fading;

Children growing, those-behind towing, new-facts knowing;

GAPP students visiting, the nervous fidgeting, Rubics-cube
widgeting;

Educators teaching, the aspiring reaching,

summarizing leeching;

Chaperones leading, adolescents pleading, good marks needing.

James R Ellerston

Beim Matheunlerricht

The variables are different in a German classroom—

But the testing of a Bernoullie experiment is the same.

A test is made with 3 questions.

Every question has 3 answers and only 1 is correct.

A person attempts to guess.

Let X be a chance variable for the number of correct answers.

Calculate the probability distribution.

But my mind drifted

to a probability experiment with only 2 players—

I thought about how Game Theory won a Nobel Prize

for its mathematician from Princeton (John Nash)

and his work at RAND with nuclear proliferation—

And so we would need 6 charts

to display the full equation of world threat,

and the number of tries

would require a longer tree to diagram.

My mind drifted

to the theory of MAD (Mutually Assured Destruction)

And how it had kept the world safe for democracy;

These probability formulas were used

     in defense department calculations of how apt

the enemy was to bomb us with atomic bombs

to determine how much to "give" in negotiations.

My mind drifted

  to how many bombs do we have to drop

  to be assured that just one will reach its target

  (to be assured of at least a greater than 50% chance);

It took 13 years of bomb dropping to get Bin Laden,

     and in the final analysis took a human with a gun.

How many attempts are required to get Kaddafi?

We have a better chance of buying Willy Wonka Bars.

  and winning the Golden Ticket.

(It's a matter of minding your p's and q's in the equation.)

James R Ellerston

Bei Herr Fesslers Musikunterricht

Musik communicates well through different cultures;

Mozart performs similarly across the shrinking world;

Dodgers desire strongly a free afternoon;

Teen-agers return reluctantly for *Musik* class;

Günther plays enthusiastically the loud claves;

Josh sings loudly a rock song;

Fessler performs technically a great improvisation;

Enthusiasm develops gradually between foreign friends;

Song unchains somehow my heart;

Rock brings happily together singing musical performers.

Poems From Travels In Three Countries

Politik

Sun shines brightly through passing clouds;

Trees rustle quietly through the open windows;

Movie plays continuously on the video player;

Students watch silently the film content;

Film shows vividly thought control;

Teens sit passively in straight-backed chairs;

Shoes are worn loosely on the students' feet;

Boys sit closely with the young girls;

Snacks are provided easily between frequent classes;

Words have sometimes the same meaning;

Glass reflects lightly the mirrored image;

Politik endangers strongly the repressed population;

Fürher empowers cruelly his strong protectors;

Temperature comforts moderately with low humidity.

James R Ellerston

Physik

Lines drawn straight or with frequent curves;

Calculators determine electronically rapid answers;

Physik teaches mathematically the wave mechanics;

Waves move through the liquid material;

Sound moves beyond the solid surface;

Waves transform the changing substances;

Lines oscillate uniformly on green chalk boards;

The teacher lectures precisely on difficult topics;

The pupil draws exactly the correct answer;

A *Frau* reads quickly a chosen problem;

Therme pool splashes a soothing background;

Windows open widely in school-room walls;

Examples develop clearly on chalk boards;

Waves modulate across in vivid drawings;

Test corrected carefully on the following day;

Questions asked directly about challenged answers;

Cap worn defiantly on a young male;

A student stares quizzically at his marked exam.

Bei den Baden-Badener Sommernächten

Trumpets squealing, dancers reeling, attention stealing;

Big-band pounding, jazz music sounding, applause resounding;

Smokers puffing, matches snuffing, the aged shuffling;

Guitarist strumming, organ humming,

rhythm-section drumming;

Singer crooning, saxophones swooning, trombonist tuning;

Stage-lights shining, guitar whining, in *Deutsch* signing,

(*Currywurst* spicing);

Beer drinking, sausages linking, sun-blind eyes blinking;

Waiters willing, customers milling, *Biergärten* filling.

Das Paradies 4

Shuttered windows, manicured lawns, smoked meats,

papered walls, dialed cell phones, tiled floors, sliced
cheeses,

mooned skies, spooned potatoes, ladled soups,
pruned hedges,

barbequed dinners, compiled schedules, recycled
refuse, married parents, jellied toast, hurried
mornings,

carbonated water, enchanted villas, embossed
napkins,

tossed salads, mossed stones, hazed views, dazed
sleeping,

miraged sunsets, garaged cars, crammed bookshelves,

shaded terraces, faded bouquets, folded awnings,

molded gelatins, climbed stairs,

welcomed guests, opened doors.

A la cathedral de Notre Dame Strassbourg

Chisled stone, stained glass, vaulted roof, shuffling feet;

hushed voices, carved organ, "Thanked" Americans,

worshipped God, buried nobles, turned woodwork,

burned candles, polished tiles, tarnished brass,

renovated windows, commemorated battles.

Schloß Heidelberg

Walls thrusted, lichen crusted,

floors dusted, tower climbed,

windows framed,tourists lamed,

statues placed, sandstone defaced,

staircases spiraled,

doors blocked, time clocked,

chapel calmed, poor almed,

banquet-hall catered, meals waitered,

stone-masons carved, peasants starved,

moat defended, tapestries mended,

cobble-stone paved, flags waved, antiquity saved,

porcelain-stove heated, collars pleated, enemies
defeated,

royalty seated,

stage-opera presented, attack prevented, warfare
demented,

guide interpreted, rain-water diverted,

parapet defended, government amended,

books scribed, nobles conspired, poem inspired,

power desired,

mind designed, past consigned, truth maligned,

tunnel secreted, law meted,

deer hunted,

river photographed,

street shopped, flip-flops flopped,

food consumed,

tour-groups shuttled,

French destroyed,

ruin preserved, architecture conserved, respect
deserved.

Internationales Oldtimer-Meeting

Chrome shines on classic automobiles;

Owners' pride glows in the buffed wax on paint;

The restorers' expertise shows trained hands.

Tanned leather upholstery conforms into formed
seats;

Flags of international diplomacy still grace the fenders

of cars that have traveled across

the distances between nations;

The ages and names of exotic manufacturers

live once more in these beauties.

The testosterone of the male is appealed to—

The shapes of the car bodies strongly suggesting

speed and sport as a lifestyle

(a vendor sells black leather jackets);

Young maidens in red hats frolic near fenders.

Precision design and machine work is under the
hoods

and kept in working mechanical order;

The Stanley Steamer could not get up its head of
steam—

Its hood propped open like a festering sore

as steam pussed from its exhaust pipe—

It could not move forward.

Mercedes-Benz celebrated 125 years—

of solidity, sport and engineering leadership,

also age and grace—

BMW move over.

(These cars look like the ones in old war movies.)

Threatening clouds and thunder made men nervous

in their stylish relaxed Panama hats;

The chilled champagne emptied its glasses quickly;

The thundering skies failed to deliver

the rain which seemed imminent.

An American-style Dixieland band entertainment

would have seemed out of place

had it not been for a solitary red 1959 Cadillac

with its thruster high fins to commemorate

the American entry into the space race—

while the Germans exported Volkswagens

to the United States by the millions.

(My Junior High English Teacher had a white 1959 Cadillac;

I had seen her finally after 43 years just two weeks earlier.)

But there was only one VW *Karmann Ghia* on display;

My boyhood dream of owning one

of these stylish but economical autos

is still an unfulfilled fantasy—

Me, the small boy growing up on an Iowa farm,

and the sunglass bedecked young dark-haired teacher

in a light-fabric summer dress and sandals

who stepped out of the steel-grey sports car

which she and brought with her from Germany,

And she had even driven that fantastic car

to our hay-blown farm that summer long past—

Which today suddenly met the present in my mind.

Spitalkirche Orgelübung

There is a balm in Gilead

filling the chapel in the garden of the school;

The many pipes are commanded by *mein Sohn*;

The sounds fill the stone-walled interior

         as sunlight is filtered through the modern colors

         of the many story-telling windows of abstract glass.

Cool air still fills this space—

The heat of the day

has not yet penetrated this sanctuary,

has not rushed in through its closed copper doors;

It is opened up each morning for visitors;

My child has found

not only the key to unlock the organ console,

But also through *Musik*,

the key to open humanity's souls.

Poems From Travels In Three Countries

Schülerkonzert mit Blockflöten
In Klosterkirche Lichtenthal

The tambourine rings as

the gamba resounds bass from the arched ceiling;

The windows of the chancel area stimulate the eyes

with shades of red, white, green, and blue;

People file in—

the voices of the mothers conversing rapidly

to the shaking of umbrellas in the back of the chapel.

The small harpsichord is in the front corner;

Its voice is easily heard in the back corner where I sit;

Sheep may never graze or soar so easily again

as when the young soprano's voice blended

with the two recorders singing out the tripled rhythms

of Bach's simple genius.

Throughout the program the statue of Mary

continued to hold the infant Jesus

from her perch to the left of the platform.

A half-sized detailed crucifix hangs over the center

of the congregation;

(The wound in His side is blood red.)

A girl now plays a bass recorder without a bocal;

(The large square angled instrument I have never before seen.)

Flourishes of running sixteenth-notes decorate the acoustics

and there is robust applause.

(Why is it that afterward when flowers are brought forward,

the guy doesn't get a bouquet of flowers?)

Orgelkonzert

The candles were lit;

The sun moved across the windows;

The organ strained the walls of the church—

but Bach did not dance.

The women next to us kept trying to tap her toe;

She could not—

and neither could I;

The mechanics were unsteady

even though a lot of notes were somehow swiftly played.

The organist had come to Baden-Baden

to practice the art of fugue playing,

and did not perform well.

In the listener there was no trance of enlightenment

and certainly no mental ecstasy.

The rhythmic pulse of God's creation

was absent to Bach's horror.

James R Ellerston

Das Kurhaus

Opulent red carpet sustains an image of graciousness,

while Ming dynasty vases suggest the world-wide appeal

of French roulette.

The Russian accent of our tour guide easily rolled off the names

of famous Casino visitors—

Dostievsky, Tolstoy, and Tschaikovsky.

Portraits on the walls suggested aristocracy of a bygone era;

The inside-joke is that the Casino is now a big money-maker—

for the state government.

The city of Baden-Baden maintains the opulent park

and floral gardens in front of the *Kurhaus*;

By evening the original gas lights grace the façade

of the building (and lend elegance by day.)

Synagogue Site in Baden-Baden

The former site of the synagogue is marked by a single stone;

The brass plaque commemorates the burning

of this house of worship 11 November 1938.

We discuss the use of the word *Kristalnacht*

and that the word is no longer used in modern Germany

(although in common usage still in American histories.)

The site of the synagogue has been turned into a parking lot

since my first visit six years ago;

Once a bare and desolate lot, preserved in a natural state,

it is now a source of parking revenue.

A stone in *Willy-Brandt Platz* marks the actual *Kristalnacht*

with a plaque and commemoration

for the absent Jews of Baden-Baden,

who were rounded up and taken away.

Raised square markers in the sidewalk in front of buildings

mark the names of Jews who were driven out

by the National Socialists in the pogrom;

The markers are of brass and shine against the pavement stones.

The only young Jew in our student group is more impressed

with the flavor of his ice cream

than our brief commemoration of these horrible crimes;

Our attempt at inclusiveness fails again—

yet others are moved to ask a question—

How could one person stand against the Nazis?

The answer is that it could be done,

and that the headmaster of our partner school did it—

standing up for the rights of his Jewish students.

His name (Leo Woleb) is proclaimed in bronze

in the front entrance of the school building.

The street around the school which bears his name,

Leo Woleb Weg (Leo Woleb Way),

is also used as a parking lot by the school faculty.

Poems From Travels In Three Countries

Basel am Montag

Our trip did not require passports;

The eyes of border and immigration people watch closely

the throngs of people leaving German trains

coming into Switzerland at the city station (*SBB*);

(No passports were needed to be shown.)

Our chaperone and guide searched hurriedly;

We went down wide avenues and narrow alleys;

We are all fallible;

A student guide rescues our group.

We find our way through a park to the *Münster*,

a darkened church with much scaffolding,

(A mixture of Romanesque and Gothic architecture).

We meet afterward outside on a broad terrace

standing above the Rhine;

The view from the top presented swimmers and sunbathers

on the steps of the opposite bank;

147

(Through the coin-operated binoculars the many women across

the water appeared too mature to appeal

to the sexual imaginations of teen-aged boys.)

A salad with chicken complimented an evening marred only

by the price of currency exchange

into a strong Swiss franc.

Maulbronn Kloster

(A U.N. World Heritage Site)

An hour's ride in a coach to a parking lot—

(Busses always park a long way from the entrance

so people are eager when they get to the ticket window.)

Our English speaking guide welcomes us in German—

(Which was OK since our group was mostly German teen-agers

along with our own American group from home.)

The broken phrases which the guide used

echoed off the stone walls and floors.

Scaffolding was everywhere—

(Our attempt to save the thousand-year-old past

requires nearly continuous restoration.)

The transition from Roman Catholic to Protestant

required reformation;

The transition from the all-boys school

(attended by Hermann Hesse)

to the present co-ed school

required a liberation

and a drive for equality for young women;

The school now admits

only twenty-five students per class.

One wonders if with the sexual-equality quotas

of modern times

whether Hermann Hesse would have been admitted at all;

His main character failed to become a prodigy

and was ground to failure Beneath the Wheel.

By any evaluation the teen-agers showed their lack of interest

in the battle between ancient monks

over the merits of Gothic or Romanesque architecture

and which type of arch was better

(since they used both types;)

The walls were thick and the windows tall;

The three tiered fountain was dry;

The students' patience waned.

Young mouths began to converse

with the intensity of peer pressure;

Young lovers took time to kiss;

Poems From Travels In Three Countries

The tour was too long,

the vaulted ceilings too cold,

the rooms damp;

The chambers were dim and dank;

Two students sat in the cold hearth of an unused fire place

The excellent acoustics of the room used for concerts

went unused by our tour guide—

(who finally had the attention of the group

once they had sunk into comfortable chairs;)

The tour guide simply said farewell;

The students then had the free time

they had been waiting for—

For some reason the playground beckoned.

James R Ellerston

Alte Meister—Junge Solisten

Baden-Badener Philharmonie

Weinbrennersaal Kurhaus

A surprise in an old room—

new seats, stage lighting, décor—

all with the traditional beautiful antique chandeliers.

The old formal palace chairs were gone;

My bottom and back could sink comfortably

into a modern foam-upholstered chrome-framed chair.

The music of Walton emerged from the young viola soloist—

strong, confident, and rich-toned—

played with complete ease and technical facility;

The orchestra evoked the harmonious pallet of Ravel.

Beethoven followed played with *bravura*—

with attention to detail, cleanness of articulation,

emphasis on dynamics;

Beethoven lived in a performance that deserved a *Bravo!*

What an enjoyable hour!

Poems From Travels In Three Countries

Orgelübung 6 Juli 2011

Entering the stone church of the city,

the antique key lets us in

but also old lock secures us in;

We climb a spiral staircase to the loft of the organ

above the back of the church;

The tones of Widor are played quietly

so that the neighboring *Frau*

can sleep until 15.00 uhr,

(the legal time for noise abatement in Baden-Baden

to allow for the old to nap.)

The great organ towers above the rear of the church,

reaching to the ceiling in lead and copper;

Mein Sohn knows the switches

and the pitches to play for the *Toccata*.

Musik is the language which grants him

a borrowed key for access

to one of the great pipe organs

in a church in Baden-Baden.

James R Ellerston

Europa Park 2011

This time we arrived by train

with a quick shuttle bus to the gate;

A hurried passing-out of tickets and we were on our way

to terrifying rides on twisted tracks of steel;

The trill of rapid acceleration, the crescendo of screams,

the pull of centrifugal force—

Add to this the darkness of space

inside a symmetrical dome—

And all the excitement in the world

could not tempt me to ride the things;

The grey-haired set of tired chaperones

and young women filled with fear

watch from the café table over *Bier und Kaffee*

by a quiet water-filled fountain.

The young, carefree, and full blooded

are turned completely upside down

emitting the overwhelming shrieks of trauma

which are normal only in a time of warfare.

Poems From Travels In Three Countries

A tiny child with his pacifier was driving

one of the miniature bumper cars;

The rides spin, the children scream

and cry out in their excitement.

I see a cancer-child wheeled past

in his high-tech wheelchair

Wearing his grey stocking hat

to cover his lack of hair;

And there is the reason why this entire

Europa Park exist at all—

Despite all the different alphabets and tastes in food—

Hope is the same in any language;

It is spelled with laughter;

It is written with a child's smile.

Sometimes our response to the challenges

that we are dealt in life

Just wants to make us scream—

and these fun machines help us to do it

without a psycho-clinic.

The Norwegian Edvard Munch was our painter of the day;

(He created the famous painting "The Scream".)

Lichtentaler Allee 16 Juli 2011

Lush green lawns spread from the side

of the paved pathway bordering the river *Oos*;

while my legs and feet take one step after another

beneath the overhanging trees;

We go past countless bridges across the water

(public and private);

We explore a rose garden;

We read menus posted on the gated communities

of exclusive hotels

(complete with card-readers for guests to utilize

to gain entrance to the lace-railed private span

leading to the security of their affluent world.)

We see the villas of the wealthy of Baden-Baden,

along with a few shirtless adolescent boys playing

in the stone-lined bottom of the river;

For a tired and worn body near day's end,

the only choice when we reach the *Kloster*,

is to ride the next bus to the city-centre for dinner.

James R Ellerston

Museum Frieder Burda
Bleckbläser des SWR Sinfonieorchesters
Baden-Baden und Freiburg

The florescent brightness of the room resembles

a sterile operating room with the exception

of the eight over-sized paintings on exhibit

on the stark white walls.

(The pictures themselves make an exhibition—

The display of the Leipzig artist Neo Raugh,

extends throughout our visit to Baden-Baden.)

The artwork consists of hardly discernible figures

which portray a bleak tortured dream world,

ascending from the depths of time

before or after the present

on which the viewer tries to ascribe

some meaning to the anguish portrayed.

One was able to sit down

in a comfortable back row seat,

an acoustic sensible distance from the eleven brass musicians

on the platform who described the pictures

at a previous expedition with the precision required

by Modest Mussorgsky,

with added accents by some adept percussionists.

The spirited brass played into our summertime evening,

challenged only by the acoustics

of a room not designed for *Musik*;

Those in the front rows

could only find humor

in the power of the playing;

These professionals merited all praise;

no one had been tempted by the arrangement

to "Send in the Clowns".

Am Marienplatz 18 Juli 2011

I am again watching people parade

past my *Bier* on the table—

the pregnant woman carrying her baby;

the pram and the stroller;

Many people are wearing jackets today—

the sky is cloudy

The rain drops easily under the umbrella

of the sidewalk restaurant table.

I am in full view of the gilded statue

tall on its monumental pillar

in front of the ornate *Rathaus* spared by the war—

its figures dancing to the folk music of Bavaria

two times per day;

This causes the people to gather and stare upward

in curiosity and amusement

with a sea of video-cameras aimed

toward the ornate neo-gothic tower

and spinning figurines.

Pigeons search the paving stones for morsels

dropped, discarded, or cast their way

by the affluent and worldly tourists on parade.

A boy walks by with bright yellow canvas shoes;

A woman walks with a chocolate-grey dog without a leash—

the dog marching obediently at her side;

Bells ring out their clang to mark the quarter-hour

from the copper-topped church tower across the square;

People move faster as the rain comes down;

I continue to hold my place at the small round table

with the un-drunk *Bier* in my glass.

A couple with no umbrella stands in the rain

and argues which direction to go;

The woman at the table next to me smokes a third cigarette;

I count the accumulation of butts in her ashtray;

Plastic shopping bags protect purchases from the rain;

whether souvenirs or necessities cost *Euro*;

Clear plastic covers protect the babies in strollers

James R Ellerston

from droplets;

People who know were they are going

hurry into the underground;

The woman carries her parasol to protect the masculinity

of her male companion's leather jacket;

He strides with manly confidence,

so oblivious to her assistance.

Riding to *Salzburg*

One young man in the compartment is sleeping;

Another reads a book in German

consulting his dictionary;

The train passing next to us creates

strobe-like patterns across his pages;

My son heads to the *Bistro* car for *Kaffee*;

Young men discuss their artistic endeavors;

The train rolls on past southern Bavarian farmsteads,

their large barns are often attached to the houses;

Church spires dominate the small towns along the tracks;

Mountains begin to appear with sharp rock outcroppings

emerging abruptly on treeless slopes.

My son stands,

camera pressed against the glass,

Snapping pictures when the breaks in the trees

allow views of the craggy vistas beyond;

Cows graze the lower slopes;

James R Ellerston

A passenger across from me tortures my stomach

by his choice of chewing on a pretzel,

oblivious in his obvious pleasure of its salty taste;

Another passenger cracks potato chips—

which he could have eaten in the *Bistro* car—

talking with his mouth chomping away;

The sharp crack of the chips sounds American

(since they stack so well in their innovative container.)

The sheltering roof of the train shed

welcomes us to Salzburg.

Poems From Travels In Three Countries

Salzburg

The water-color painters still gather in the yard

surrounding the cathedral in its Baroque majesty.

Mirabel Gardens, acres of flowers in formal design,

with its fountain spread out in do-re-mi splendor,

graced the front of the palace.

The formidable *Burg* above the city

was never conquered by outside forces,

It survived better than the cathedral

(with its vast dome requiring fifteen years of rebuilding

following a 1945 aerial bomb.)

The students sat in the rear church pews,

(bored after ten minutes of viewing,)

their teen-stomachs calling them to lunch

(so short a period after morning tea time.)

Filled with lunch we are off in our climb to the *Burg*,

dominating the view from the city,

and providing aerial landscapes of the city

from its ramparts.

Film "The Wave" *Die Welle*

Autocracy, anarchy, democracy, rebellion, autocrats, Nazis, again?
Neo-Nazis, skepticism, unhappiness, intellectual, surveillance,
intelligentsia, control, ideology, minority withdrawal, *Füher*, violence,
group coercion, gang action, group conformity, defamation,
discipline (is power) desertion, social injustice, exclusion, high
unemployment, newspaper, media, inflation, internet, extreme
nationalism, image of power, peer pressure, firepower, sport,
weapons, harassment, leader worship, redemption, pamphlets against,
un-information, propaganda, unity, uniforms, uniformity, burning the
old way, name, for group, logo, action is power, protection,
replacement "family".

"The Wave" ended with a bang;

The protesting student was shot;

Like many in a failed dictatorial movement

the young activist put a pistol to his mouth,

un-reconciled to the failure of the movement;

The teacher, for inciting the students to organize,

which caused two deaths,

was hauled away by the *Polizei*.

Poems From Travels In Three Countries

Deutche Bahn nach München

The train turns eastward towards western Bavaria;

Passing through *Ulm* and *Augsburg*,

The students, centered on themselves or their peers,

do not see the countryside

or the industrial base of Germany

(with its backside turned to the many electrified tracks;)

Instead the students see the inside of their eyelids,

their books, text messages on cell phones,

and applications on their I-pods (games);

Mein Sohn stares at the inexhaustible screen of his laptop;

I purchase a *Kaffee*;

The train whines on at high speed,

Racing through the south of this highly developed land;

The next destination is *München*.

James R Ellerston

At the Base Village of *Schloss Neuschwanstein*

The train bumped along with ten stops

in small undistinguishable Bavarian villages,

each with its *Bahnhof* in disrepair;

People stood on platforms as if on a movie set,

and moved as the train approaches

as if given a cue for the drama of German life.

The bus transfer dropped us in the tourist village

at the base of the mountain;

The dark forest towered above us as we dashed through the rain

into one busy souvenir shop after another;

People crowded restaurant tables,

as much to fill the time before their ascent and tour,

as to find a place out of the rain,

and to obtain food.

I try to eat my *Apfelstrudel* slowly

with *Kaffee und Milch*;

Time must be passed while the more able-bodied climb

168

Poems From Travels In Three Countries

the slopes of the pinnacle and descend the spiral stairs

of turrets and kingly halls;

Meanwhile there was a parade of colored umbrellas—

yellow, green and black;

Rain continued to fall heavily.

Tour busses climbed the hills of the tourist village,

their gears grinding, with advertising signs for Austria

and of course Bavaria;

The busses idled their engines impatiently at the bus stop,

and the drivers honked their horns

while trying to jockey the bus into position

at the pick up point to sell tickets,

And to transfer people back for the train to civilization.

I had given away my umbrella to my son,

who needed it leading the expedition up the mountain;

They would return cold and wet;

Some of them were not dressed for the coolness of the weather

which has been so unusual this trip;

There were men with families on the street,

and a blind women with a white cane;

A lady in an overcoat carried a floral patterned umbrella;

I saw a plaid umbrella and the women wore a raincoat;

A women ran behind her babies stroller—

her umbrella perched to keep the child dry.

Women dashed between the restaurant and the *Toilette*,

trying to avoid the soaking downpour;

The blind lady with the white cane and her friend came and

took a seat at my table within the restaurant's warmth;

I found them interesting excuses to sit longer at the table

as they ordered and consumed their desserts.

Car tires swished on the wet street,

and people continued to gather at the bus stop.

Men wore warm jackets

with hoods pulled up over their heads;

The tops of the cliffs were shrouded in fog—

and our group wasn't back down the mountain yet;

The questions were—

What will our bus time be?

Our train time back?

And there would not be much in *München* tonight

except for a group meal together at the *Hofbräuhaus*.

Dachau **Memorial Site**

The wires rusted on the insulators on the high fence;

The trench barricaded with depth before the wire on the inside;

If one survived being shot in the barbed wire on the ground,

The electrified fence would have finished one off.

Of course the system in time would have worked

its incessant inhumanity on one's mind;

The lack of privacy, the threat of punishment,

and crowded conditions in the barracks

would have made for sleepless nights—

with dreams punctuated by the barks of killer dogs.

Today our shoes crushed misery and ash amongst the gravel;

We counted the foundations of the thirty barracks;

We paid homage in the newly built Jewish memorial;

We visited the crematorium and room for the dead (bodies).

Our only Jewish traveler observed the Hebrew writing

and the ignorance of his peers about the Jewish place

Poems From Travels In Three Countries

in this camp's window into a dark period of history;

We were careful to also mention gypsies and homosexuals;

We passed a Catholic chapel,

with an array of unlit candles about and on the altar.

A modern cafeteria was filled with warm food;

Our group sat around the table in a quick return to daily reality;

French fries were on our American plates;

The students ordered differently, *lasagna* mixed with *Schnitzel*.

We browsed the book-store, searching for English books,

but most titles were in German;

We boarded the crowded bus back to Dachau *Bahnhof*

and rode the train back to *München*;

After a view into horror,

the teen-agers wanted only free time—

not to be fenced in by rules or imprisoned by a curfew.

James R Ellerston

Schloss Nymphenburg

Once again the gliding swans captured the students' attention

as we walked under umbrellas along the curved drives;

We were issued *Kinder* tickets by mistake,

but they were not the correct admission

to view the regal carriages and sleighs;

Anyway the rain had dampened the desire of the young people

to pay another *Euro* 4.50

in order to view more gold gilt and splendor.

The Baroque opulence of the place—

the endlessly curving moldings in plaster,

nude cherubs, ceiling paintings, and upholstered walls—

For the group was not as alluring as time with teen-aged peers

within the four flat walls of hotel rooms.

Poems From Travels In Three Countries

Final: Leaving *Deutschland*

We are greeted by yet another overcast morning;

Up early, a hurried breakfast, a quick walk to the train station;

Car twenty-two was an entire platform down the train;

The ride was swift and smooth on the *ICE*

speeding through the south German countryside.

A quick loading of the plane,

and we were on our way home—

To familiarity, to family, to security.

to home.

James R Ellerston

Türkische Mosque im Deutschland

greeted by words of Arabic carvings on a broad wooden door;

finding inside stone steps for ritualized washing—

removal of shoes, washing of the feet—

preparing cleanliness of spirit,

for holy prayer in the segregated prayer room

(women are kept apart delegated to the gallery

observing the barefoot and kneeling men in prayer);

all bodies to be folded toward Mecca

on their own allocated square of carpeting

beneath the painted dome and colorful crystal chandelier;

coverings in tiles of blue guard all four walls

to quiet the spirit within,

but excite the person observing for the first time

the chamber with its pulpits

for thoughts central to the life

of *mein Freund*, a Muslim of *Türkische* ancestry.

Poems From Travels In Three Countries

SWR Orckestra im Festspielhaus

the orchestra purposely poised in brightly lit positioned form,

staged, led in flight by an able conductor's craft;

it soared air-borne in colors of *timbre* combined—

difficult ideas in sound first heard in the mind of genius,

twisted notions of the romanticist Nietzsche

notated spatially on inked staves and pages—

printed paper outlines of manuscript beauty;

now reconstituted rising over time and interval aloft,

performed by specialist technicians on their tools—

instruments of highly crafted design

and standardized acoustical excellence

providing an accuracy of cyclic pitch benefited

from years of practical experience and repeated effort,

by years of practice at the musical art—

presenting the cognition of one man,

grave dead but now alive in our present time—

such sonic ideas void of principles of religion or philosophy;

thoughts divorced from the *politik* of the previous period of
conception,

and present time of chaos and rebellion and competing audible
realization—

these ideas now spread out before eager ears and alert minds,

stimulating the finest imagination in listeners,

and giving freedom from pathos and tormented ideals

in the lives of the participant audience.

CHECK OUT JAMES' OTHER BOOK, AVAILABLE ON AMAZON TODAY!

Made in the USA
Lexington, KY
06 November 2019